Shimmer
ART

by the editors of Klutz

KLUTZ®

Make a shimmering, sparkling work of art!

Start with a bag of fabulous, oh-so-fancy sequins in a rainbow of colors—and end with art you can display that shines and twinkles whenever a gentle breeze passes by.

This book shows you how to use special flat sequins, called *paillettes* (pie-YETS) as well as Klutz-exclusive custom-made sequin shapes. Mix and match them however you like to create a mesmerizing masterpiece that's totally you.

Sound like fun?

Then it's time to get your sparkle on!

This is a paillette.

Contents

Rainbow • 25

Ball gown • 27

Butterfly • 29

Hot air balloon • 31

Owl • 33

Groovy girl • 35

Peacock • 37

Unicorn • 39

Peace sign • 41

Dress form • 43

Heart • 45

Sea horse • 47

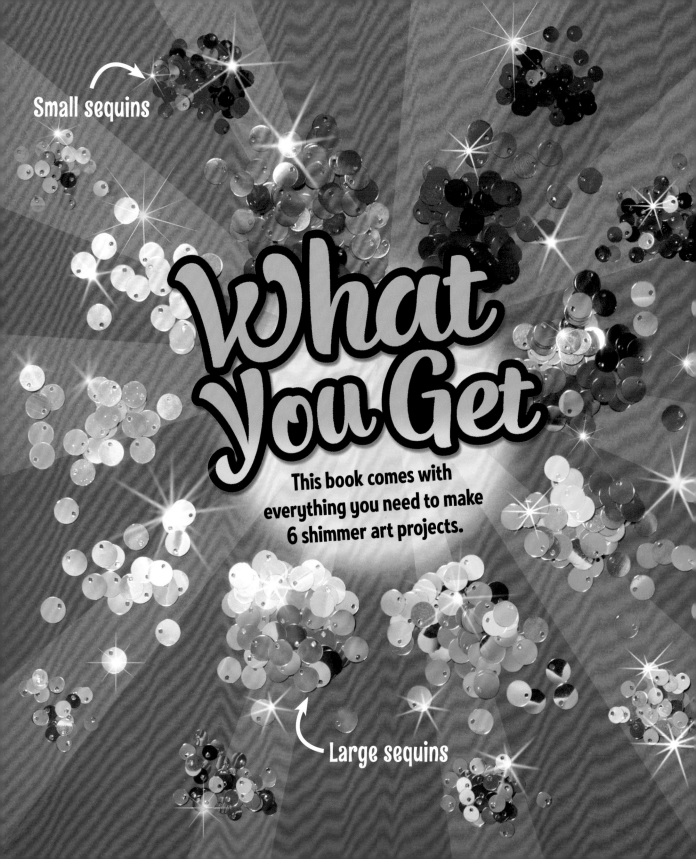

Small sequins

What You Get

This book comes with everything you need to make 6 shimmer art projects.

Large sequins

740 pins

Custom pin-pushing and sequin picker-upper tool

12 pattern papers

12 custom sequins

6 project boards

You'll also need:
- Clear tape
- Scissors
- Black permanent marker

2 display stands

THE Basics

Love

PATTERNS

(pages 25-47)

There are 12 patterns, so choose your favorites first to decorate the 6 boards in the box.

Each pattern is very simple to use, just follow the color guides.

● **Pink dot** = large sequin

● **Blue dot** = small sequin

● **Green dot** = just a pin (no sequin)

Custom sequins

There are 9 projects that use custom sequins. Line up the specialty sequins with the outlines on the pattern papers, and use the dots as a reference to place the pins.

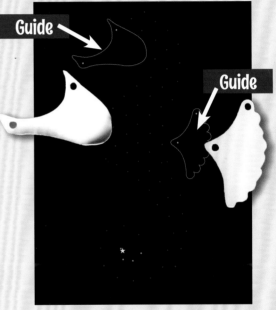

Guide

Guide

Starting point

Each pattern has a yellow star by one of the dots. This is where you place your first pin. Sometimes you'll want to pin sequins in a specific direction, so double-check the pattern page for additional instructions before you begin.

Love

Starting point

There is a sequin count for each project in the corner of the page. Don't worry, you'll have enough sequins to make all 6 boards, but you might want to plan where to use your favorite colors before they run out.

WRAPPING THE BOARDS

Whether your design is tall or short, you cover the board the same way.

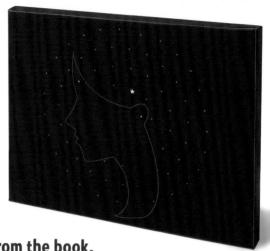

Carefully remove the entire pattern page from the book.

1 Using scissors, cut around the pattern on the dashed lines. Place the picture side up and fold along all of the scored lines.

2 Keeping the dot side down, place a board onto the middle rectangle of the pattern.

3 Fold over the rounded flaps first, then tape them to the board.

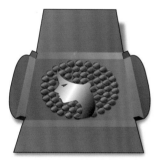

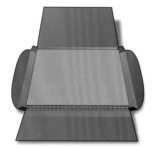

4 Press in the tiny flaps on one side so they rest against the edges of the board . . .

Flap— —Flap

5 . . . then fold the long flap over and tape it.

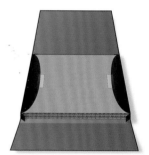

Repeat on the other edge for a neatly wrapped project board.

Done!

Now it's time to make your sequin selections.

SEQUINS

Before you start, pour your sequins into a small bowl or storage container.

Pick your colors

There are 6 colors to design with, plus a few extra holographic and pastel sequins to use as accents.

Custom sequins

Check the pattern! You'll pin these large silver sequins in one of two ways:

- ⬤ = Pin the custom sequin by itself

- ⬤ or ⬤ = Pin the custom sequin behind another sequin

NOT SURE WHICH COLORS TO USE?

Plan out your design by laying the sequins down on the board before you pin. If you're a sequin artist with a vision, just pick and pin as you go. See pages 14-19 for some color inspiration. **You really can't go wrong with sparkle!**

Sequin picker-upper

- Use the sticky ball end of the tool to pick up the colored sequins you want to use.

- Store the tool in a plastic bag so the sticky side doesn't get dirty or lose its stickiness.

- If it does lose its stickiness, just run it under some cold water and let it dry.

PINNING THE BOARD

You need the pin-pushing side of the tool for this job.

1 Carefully slide a pin into the hole of a sequin.

2 Holding the sequin and pinhead with your fingers, poke the pin through a dot on the pattern paper and push it into the board, just enough so it won't fall out.

Try to make the pins stand straight up.	This is a little too wobbly!

You can also use the indentation on the tool to push in the pins partway.

3 Holding the pin steady and upright, put the pin-pushing tool over it . . .

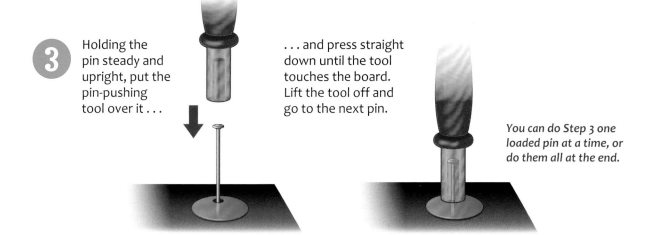

. . . and press straight down until the tool touches the board. Lift the tool off and go to the next pin.

You can do Step 3 one loaded pin at a time, or do them all at the end.

4 After you insert all the pins, check that they're all the same height by looking at your board from the side.

If some pinheads are higher than others, use the tool to push them down until they all line up.

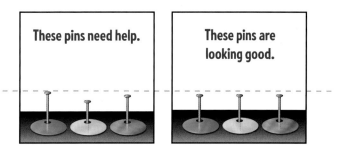

These pins need help.

These pins are looking good.

Handle pins with care

- Work on a flat table when you're inserting pins. Don't work with the board on your lap.

- If a pin gets stuck in the pin-pushing tool, ask an adult to help get it out.

- Throw out any bent pin and use a new one.

- If a pin pokes out the back of the board, pull the pinhead up from the front until the pin no longer pokes out.

- Put pins away when you're not using them and keep them away from kids under 10 years old.

- If a pin poke does break your skin, wash and bandage the area.

- Carefully pick up and throw away all the pieces of any broken pin immediately.

SHOW OFF YOUR SHINE

There are two different-sized display stands, but they work the same way.

The longer stand is for the wide boards.

The shorter stand is for the tall boards.

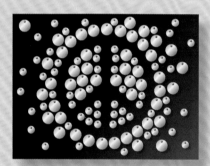

Final touch-ups

Before you attach the display stand, check to make sure you're happy with your art.

To remove large fingerprints from the custom sequins, gently rub them away with a microfiber cloth (the type of cloth used to clean a computer screen) or a cosmetic cotton pad (use the soft, smoother side).

It's impossible to remove all the fingerprints from the little sequins—but don't worry, they will still sparkle brightly!

To fix scratches on the pattern papers, lightly run a black permanent marker over the top of them.

How to build your display stands

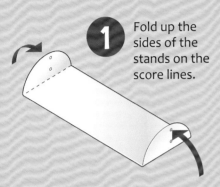

1 Fold up the sides of the stands on the score lines.

2 On the side of your finished board, carefully center the stand's holes on the side of the board.

With your fingers, push a pin through the bottom hole all the way into the side of the board.

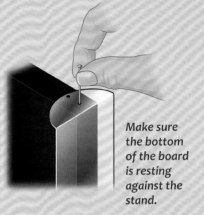

Make sure the bottom of the board is resting against the stand.

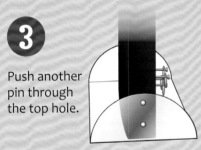

3 Push another pin through the top hole.

4 Repeat Steps 2–3 on the other side.

5 Once the stand is pinned, tilt the board forward so all the sequins slide to the pinheads.

Slowly tilt the board upright. The sequins should dangle at the ends of the pins.

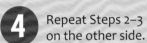

If you have any stubborn sequins that stick to the board, gently blow on the sequins or tap the back of the board to set them free.

Ooh! Aah!

Try putting your fabulous design near a window. The breeze will make the sequins shimmer and sway.

GET
Inspired

No two sequins shine the same, and no two shimmer art projects need to look the same! Browse through the next few pages for inspiration.

Try your design in one color.

Remember, if you're making art with only one color, it's easy to use up your favorite sequins fast!

Sparkle with two colors . . . or three . . .

To get the perfect balance of colors, select the sequins you want to use and mix them together in a bowl. Then let the sequin picker-upper decide your fate. Whichever sequin it picks up is the color you pin next. Don't think too much about it, just let your sequin Zen take over.

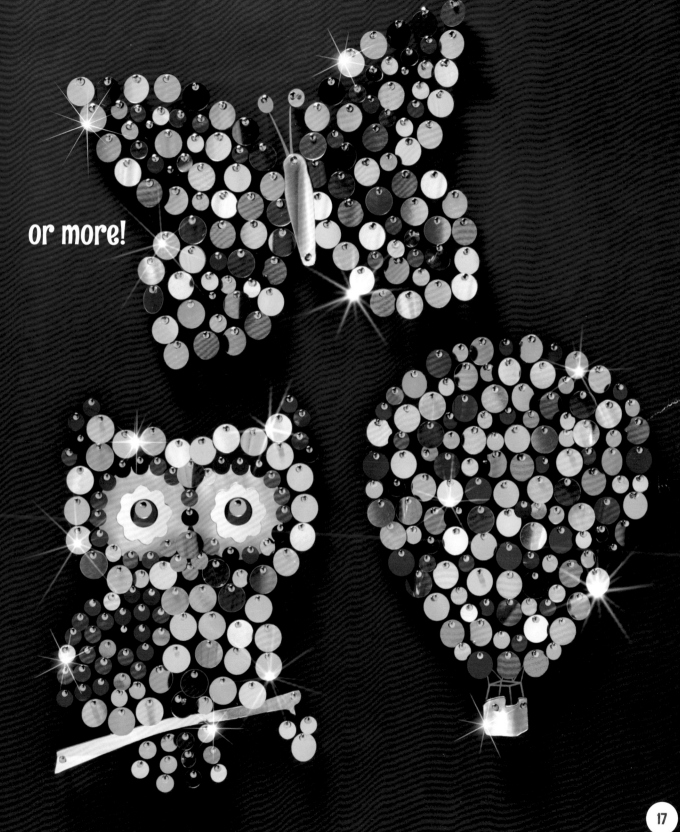

or more!

Shine with rainbow colors.

Love

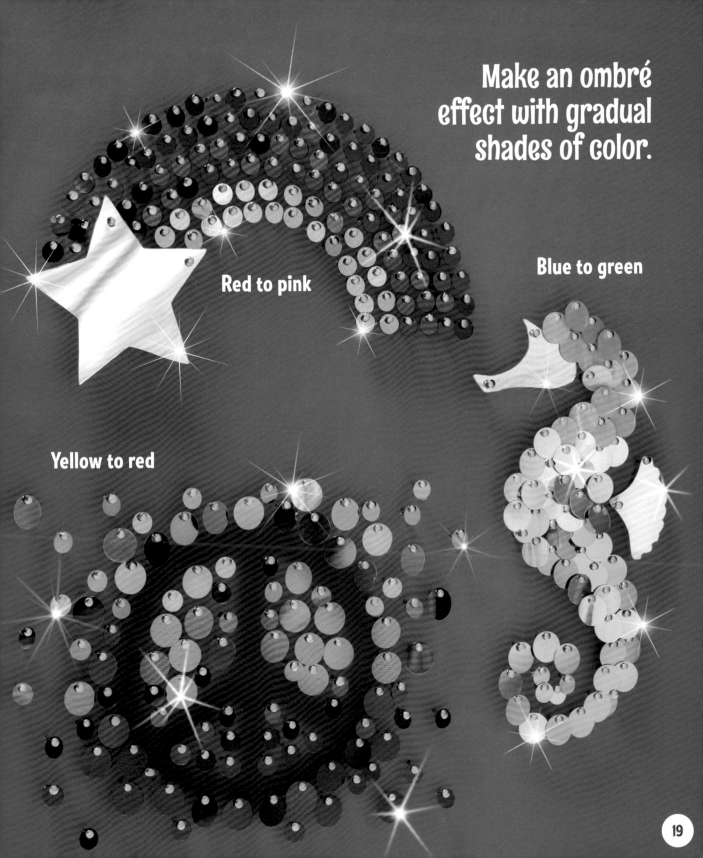

Make an ombré effect with gradual shades of color.

Red to pink

Blue to green

Yellow to red

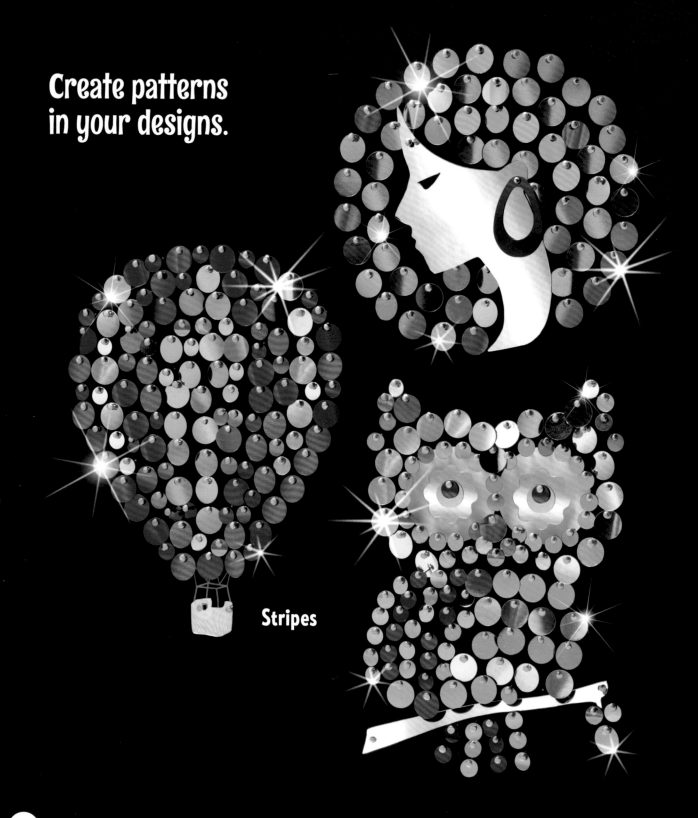

Create patterns in your designs.

Stripes

20

Polka dots

Make up your own patterns

Add some glitz to the simple backgrounds.

If you don't have a pattern to follow, or if you're adding extra paillettes around your design, it's best to lay out the sequins before you pin. That way if you change your mind, you won't have empty pinholes on your board.

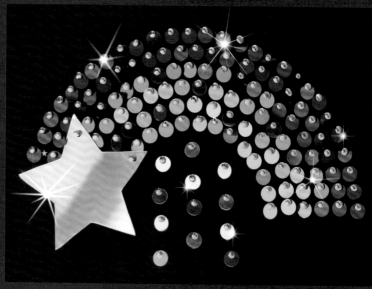

Sprinkled with sparkle

Blow some bubbles

Add borders or pretty accents

Sequin Your Life

You don't have to use the patterns included in this book to make stunning sequin pictures. Print out your favorite photo on computer paper or use a page from a magazine and glue it on top of a covered board. Let your imagination go wild!

Shimmering cities

Fabulous fashions

Sequin snowman

Pretty paillette parrot

Make a mini marquee

Sparkling sprinkles

THE Patterns

24

RAINBOW

Use this custom sequin:

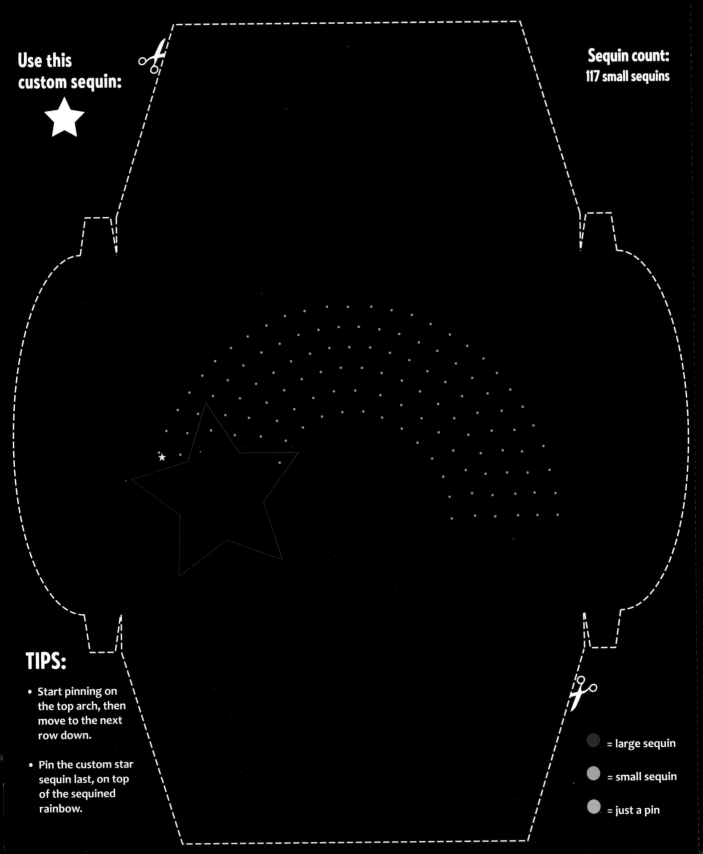

TIPS:

- Start pinning on the top arch, then move to the next row down.

- Pin the custom star sequin last, on top of the sequined rainbow.

⬤ = large sequin

⬤ = small sequin

⬤ = just a pin

BALL GOWN

Use this custom sequin:

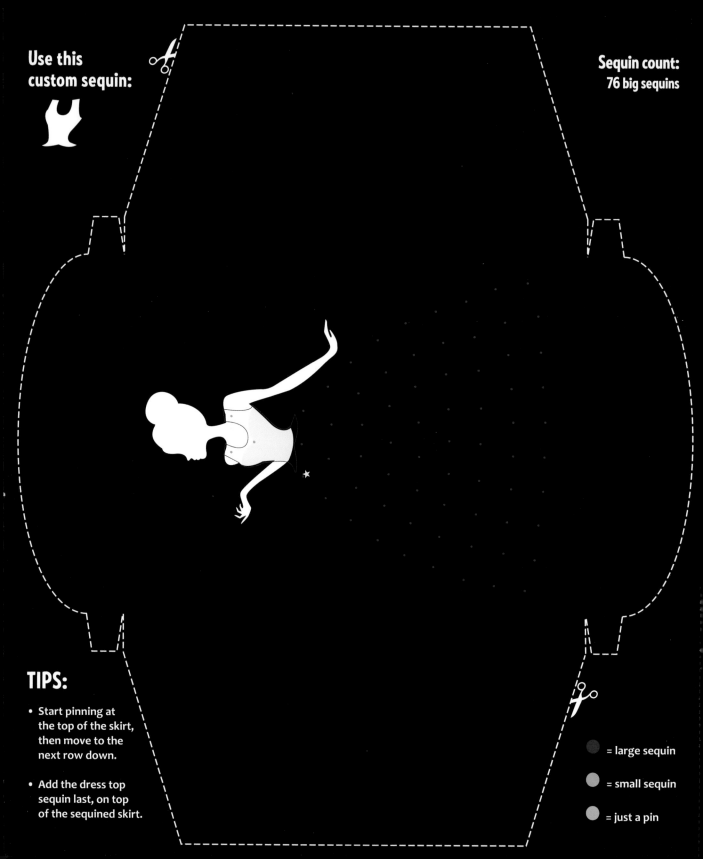

TIPS:

- Start pinning at the top of the skirt, then move to the next row down.

- Add the dress top sequin last, on top of the sequined skirt.

⬤ = large sequin

⬤ = small sequin

⬤ = just a pin

BUTTERFLY

Use this custom sequin:

TIPS:

- Start pinning on the outside of the wings, and work toward the middle.

- For a symmetrical design, complete one side first and then duplicate your colors on the other wing.

- Pin the butterfly's body sequin last, on top of the butterfly's wings.

● = large sequin

● = small sequin

● = just a pin

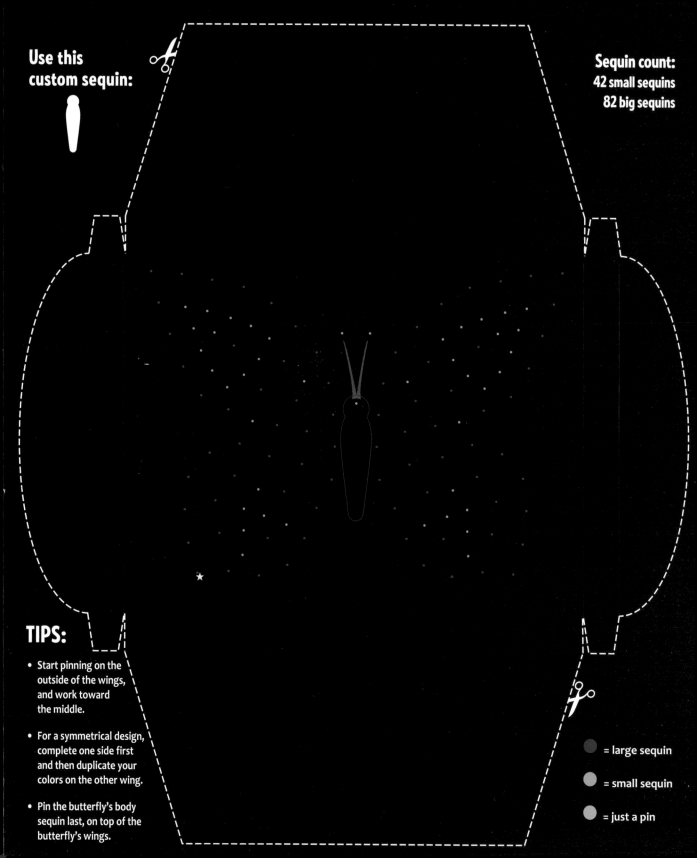

DRESS FORM

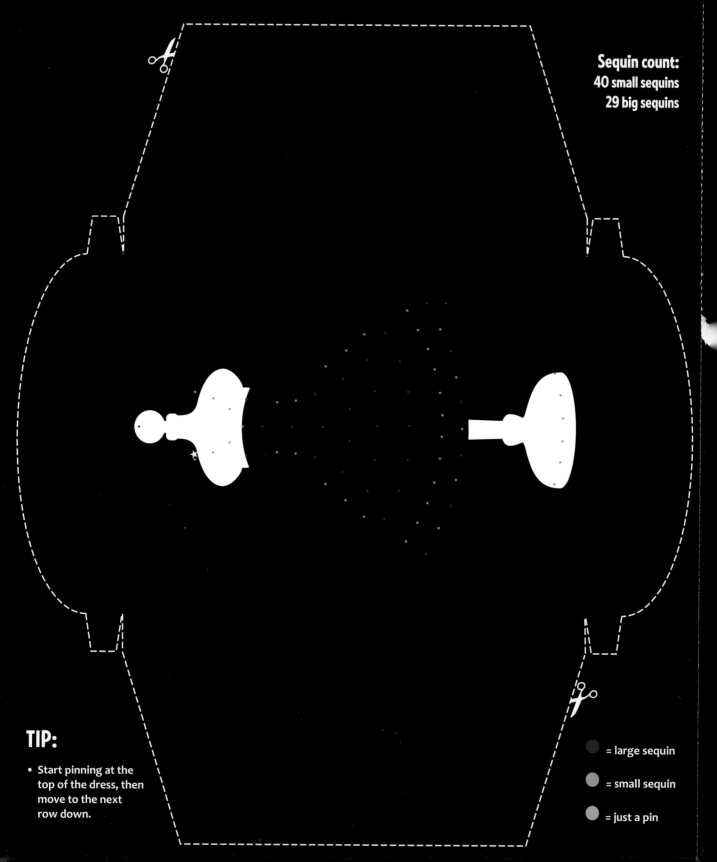

Sequin count:
40 small sequins
29 big sequins

TIP:
• Start pinning at the top of the dress, then move to the next row down.

= large sequin

= small sequin

= just a pin

Love

HEART

Love

TIP:

• Start pinning in the center, then work your way out.

= large sequin

= small sequin

= just a pin